What is the Family Proclamation?

Written by Amy Clements
Illustrated by Kimball Clements

For Oleana, Isaac, and all my future grandchildren.

———◆○◆———

Copyright © 2023 by Amy Clements

All rights reserved.

No part of this publication may be reproduced, distributed, or transmitted in any form or by any means, including photocopying, recording, or other electronic or mechanical methods, without the prior written permission of the publisher, except as permitted by U.S. copyright law. For permission requests, contact Amy Clements at acamylou@gmail.com.

The story, all names, characters, and incidents portrayed in this production are fictitious. No identification with actual persons (living or deceased), places, buildings, and products is intended or should be inferred.

This material is neither made, provided, approved, nor endorsed by Intellectual Reserve, Inc. or The Church of Jesus Christ of Latter-day Saints. Any content or opinions expressed, implied or included in or with the material are solely those of the owner and not those of Intellectual Reserve, Inc. or The Church of Jesus Christ of Latter-day Saints.

Book Cover by Kimball Clements & Rylee Witbeck

Illustrations by Kimball Clements

Art Design by Rylee Witbeck

1st edition 2023

LCCN 2023919922 | ISBN 979-8-218-30106-4

Spanish Fork, Utah

The Family: A Proclamation to the World

This proclamation was read by President Gordon B. Hinckley as part of his message at the General Relief Society Meeting held September 23, 1995, in SLC, Utah

No one has a perfect family, and that's **perfectly okay.**

We just **try** to be better **each and every day.**

"Hey Dad, what is the Family Proclamation?"

Dad smiled. "That's a great question, Lily! I would love to talk about it with you."

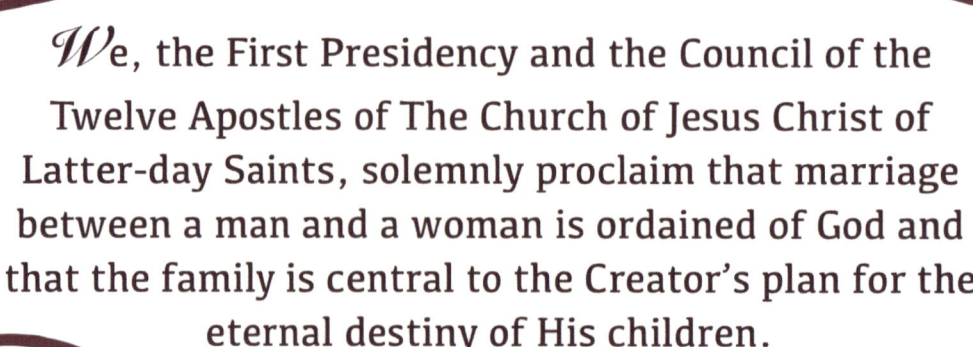

We, the First Presidency and the Council of the Twelve Apostles of The Church of Jesus Christ of Latter-day Saints, solemnly proclaim that marriage between a man and a woman is ordained of God and that the family is central to the Creator's plan for the eternal destiny of His children.

"Before you were born," Dad began, "Heavenly Father had an awesome plan to help you to become like him. Someday, he wants you to have what he has and be happy. Just like I'm your dad and I want you to be happy. He sent us to families because that is the best way to learn about being like our Heavenly Parents. After we die, we can still be with our family forever."

"Our theology begins with Heavenly parents. Our highest aspiration is to be like them."
—Dallin H. Oaks, "Apostasy and Restoration," Ensign, May 1995, 84

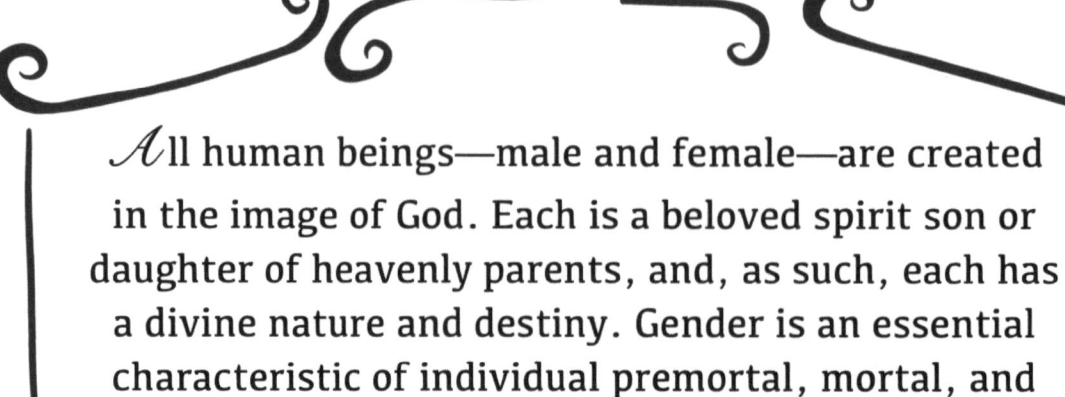

> All human beings—male and female—are created in the image of God. Each is a beloved spirit son or daughter of heavenly parents, and, as such, each has a divine nature and destiny. Gender is an essential characteristic of individual premortal, mortal, and eternal identity and purpose.

"Did you know that you have a Heavenly Father and Mother? They love you so much," Dad explained. "God created each one of us. Being a girl or a boy is very important."

Dad ruffled Lily's hair. "You were born a girl, and that means you were a girl before you came to earth and you will be a girl forever and ever. Same thing for your brother; He will always be a boy."

"Are boys better than girls?" Lily wondered.

"No sweetie," said Dad, "and girls aren't better than boys either. God loves us all the same. He sent both boys and girls to this earth to do important things. Sometimes we are called to do different things, but they are equally valuable. Can you think of some similarities and differences between girls and boys?"

"Boys and girls are both smart," Lily said. "They are both hard workers."

"That's for sure!" Dad agreed.

"Only girls can have babies," Lily continued.

"That's right—Having babies is an important job that God has given to women. What about boys?"

"Boys pass the sacrament in church, and give me blessings of healing when I'm sick."

Dad nodded. "Exactly. Our Heavenly Father has given men the responsibility to hold the priesthood. God needs both women and men in order for his plan to work. Being a girl is great, and so is being a boy."

In the premortal realm, spirit sons and daughters knew and worshipped God as their Eternal Father and accepted His plan by which His children could obtain a physical body and gain earthly experience to progress toward perfection and ultimately realize their divine destiny as heirs of eternal life.

"Did I really know God before I was born?" asked Lily.

"Yes, you did, and when he presented his plan to all of his children, we got to choose whether or not to follow his plan," said Dad.

"Did I choose to follow his plan?"

"You sure did, because you are here on earth with your very own body. Everyone who chose God's plan gets to come to earth, receive a body, and have the chance to make good choices so that one day they can live with God again."

The divine plan of happiness enables family relationships to be perpetuated beyond the grave. Sacred ordinances and covenants available in holy temples make it possible for individuals to return to the presence of God and for families to be united eternally.

"So then we can be a family forever?" Lily asked.

"That's right!" Dad exclaimed. "God wants us to be happy forever with those we love. But it's not easy. God has shown us certain steps we have to take in order to get there."

"Steps? Like a path?"

"Exactly. We call it the covenant path."

"The covenant path? What's that?" asked Lily.

Dad explained, "The covenant path guides the choices you make to live like Jesus and follow his example. It's a journey we take in our life to return to God. The first step is to be baptized."

"Hey, I was just baptized!" Lily said with excitement.

"The next step for both boys and girls is to prepare yourselves to enter the temple," Dad went on.

"I love the temple!" Lily said. "I have a picture of the temple in my bedroom, and we drive by the temple on our way to Grandma and Grandpa's house. I want to stay on the covenant path so I can go inside someday."

"That's a great plan! Temples are so important. In the temple, we participate in something called ordinances and make special promises called covenants. Going to the temple often helps us to stay on the covenant path, reach our full potential, and live with God for eternity."

"And get married!" Lily said with a grin.

"Yes, that's another step on the covenant path," Dad agreed. "When a man and a woman get married in the temple, they are sealed for all eternity, and their children are sealed to them forever and ever."

We further declare that God has commanded that the sacred powers of procreation are to be employed only between man and woman, lawfully wedded as husband and wife.

"Dad, what does 'multiply and replenish the earth' mean?"

"That means that after a man and woman are married, God wants them to have children," Dad explained. "God loves all of his children and he wants them to be able to come to earth to receive a body.

Dad continued, "When a man and woman are married, they make a commitment to each other and to God. This helps create a stable home for God to send his children."

"It is also important to know that some people want to be married and have children, but for certain reasons, they haven't received those blessings yet," Dad said. "God still loves them and knows they are striving to keep his commandments. They still have very important work on this earth."

> We declare the means by which mortal life is created to be divinely appointed. We affirm the sanctity of life and of its importance in God's eternal plan.

"What is the sanctity of life?" asked Lily.

Dad replied, "Every life is important to God, from before our birth all the way till the end of our time here on earth. Life is a gift from God and we should treasure it."

Husband and wife have a solemn responsibility to love and care for each other and for their children. "Children are an heritage of the Lord" (Psalm 127:3).

"You and mom love each other." Lily couldn't help but smile.

Dad smiled back. "Yes we do, but our relationship takes work. Sometimes we have disagreements and struggles. Every day we try to put God and each other first."

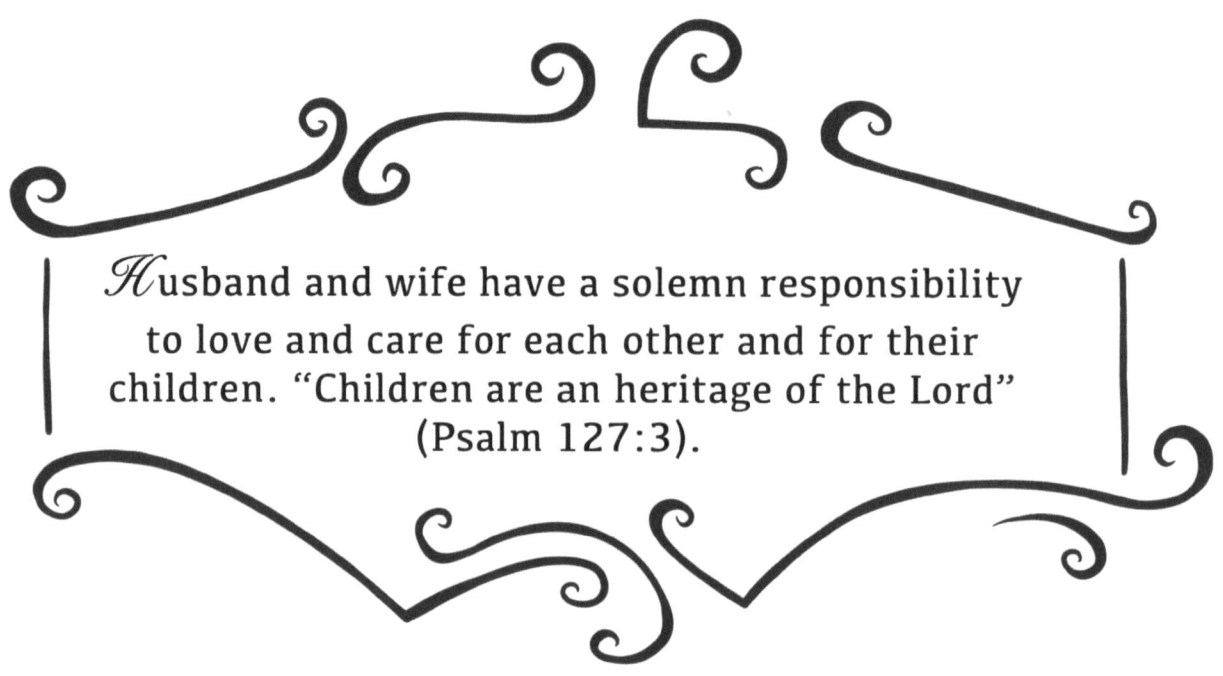

"And me too?" asked Lily.

"Of course, we love you and your brother so much! You are a special gift from God."

Parents have a sacred duty to rear their children in love and righteousness, to provide for their physical and spiritual needs, and to teach them to love and serve one another, observe the commandments of God, and be law-abiding citizens wherever they live. Husbands and wives—mothers and fathers—will be held accountable before God for the discharge of these obligations.

"I'm glad that you are my dad and that Mom is my mom," Lily said.

Dad nodded. "Moms and dads have an important responsibility. Sometimes I make mistakes, but I'm trying my best to be a good dad."

"You play kickball with me, and you and mom take me to church. We also have family prayer and read the scriptures together. Sometimes you forget, so I have to remind you."

"I'm glad I have you to remind me." Dad put a hand on Lily's shoulder.

"Remember when mom helped me make cookies for my friend when she was sad?" Lily asked.

"I sure do," replied Dad. "It makes Heavenly Father so happy when we do kind things for other people. Every person on this earth is a child of God, and he loves them all."

The family is ordained of God. Marriage between man and woman is essential to His eternal plan. Children are entitled to birth within the bonds of matrimony, and to be reared by a father and a mother who honor marital vows with complete fidelity.

"God created us so that it takes a man and a woman to have children," Dad explained. "He wants little children to have a mom and a dad to take care of them. That's why marriage is so important in God's plan."

Dad went on, "Sometimes kids don't get to live with both their mom and dad, but Heavenly Father loves all of his children and will give them extra help."

"God loves us so much that he has given us a recipe for a happy family," Dad said. "The ingredients are...
- Faith
- Prayer
- Repentance
- Forgiveness
- Respect
- Love
- Compassion
- Work
- and Wholesome recreational activities.

When we center our family on our Savior, Jesus Christ, we can't go wrong."

𝓑y divine design, fathers are to preside over their families in love and righteousness and are responsible to provide the necessities of life and protection for their families. Mothers are primarily responsible for the nurture of their children. In these sacred responsibilities, fathers and mothers are obligated to help one another as equal partners. Disability, death, or other circumstances may necessitate individual adaptation. Extended families should lend support when needed.

Dad explained, "Heavenly Father has given me the family responsibility to preside, provide, and protect."

"What does that mean, Dad?"

"It means that he wants me to lead our family back to God. He also trusts me to work hard so that our family has the things we need, and to be brave and keep danger away from our family.

"What has God asked Mom to do?" asked Lily.

"Your mom has been given special gifts from God that enable her to guide, teach, and care for our family with wisdom and compassion," Dad replied, and Lily nodded.

Dad went on, "But we can't fulfill our responsibilities alone. We walk side by side to help each other and make decisions together."

"I want to have a happy family, but sometimes my brother and I don't get along," Lily admitted.

"We are not a perfect family," Dad said, "but the important part is that we try to follow Jesus Christ. And when we make mistakes, we can repent and do better."

"I'm going to try being nice to my brother, even if he draws all over my schoolwork."

"You are definitely doing your part to help us have a successful family, just like your brother, Mom, and me."

"You work hard everyday, Dad. I'll bet if there were any monsters under the bed, you would save me."

"No monsters can get past me. And if they did, I'm sure your mom would take care of them."

We warn that individuals who violate covenants of chastity, who abuse spouse or offspring, or who fail to fulfill family responsibilities will one day stand accountable before God. Further, we warn that the disintegration of the family will bring upon individuals, communities, and nations the calamities foretold by ancient and modern prophets.

"God cares so much for all of his children," Dad said, putting an arm around Lily. "He never wants anyone to be hurt or treated badly."

"What does 'disintegration of the family' mean?" Lily frowned.

"The world tries to tell us that marriage and family no longer matter. Many people say that having a father in the home is not important, or that because not all families have a mom, dad and children together, then we shouldn't try to reach that goal."

Dad went on, "There are times when a mom or dad might make a choice that pulls a family apart. Sometimes bad choices cause other family members to suffer, even when they're not at fault. When that happens, God still loves those people, and sends his spirit to spread happiness in that family, even when they are not together.

"He even loves those who made the wrong choice," Dad continued, "and helps them to repent and return to him. The Atonement of Jesus Christ makes it possible to change our lives for the better."

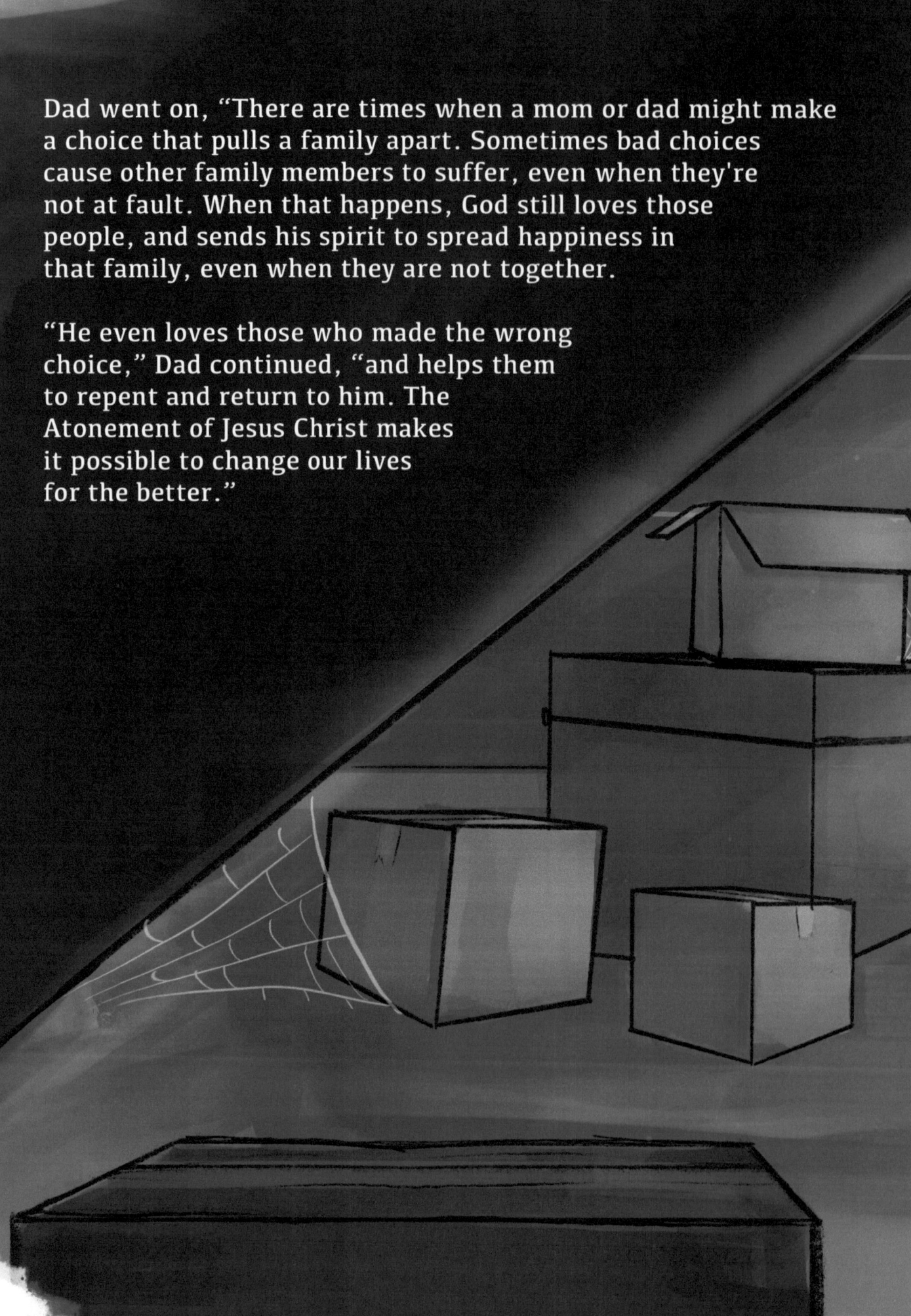

Lily became thoughtful. "I don't want our family to disin... disinte... to fall apart."

"We've got to do our best to make sure that doesn't happen," Dad agreed.

"How, Dad?"

"Remember? We can start by following God's recipe for a happy family, and always center our lives on Jesus Christ. Even when we are struggling, we should never give up on our family because God never gives up on us."

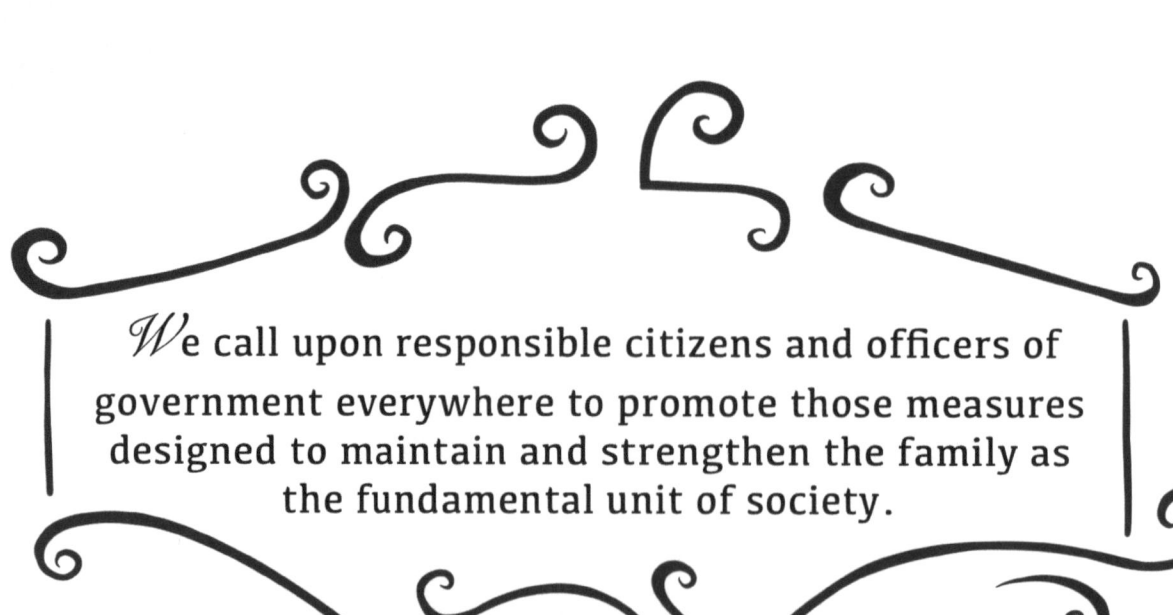

We call upon responsible citizens and officers of government everywhere to promote those measures designed to maintain and strengthen the family as the fundamental unit of society.

"What do you think we can do to strengthen families in our communities and in our country?" Dad asked.

"Maybe you should be the president, Dad!"

Dad laughed. "Maybe not the president, but we can pray for our president and government leaders. We can also vote for people that will be brave and stand for families. When families are strong, then countries are strong."

"Maybe someday I should be the president," Lily said.

"I would definitely vote for you."

"But most of all, Dad, I want to have a family that stays together forever and ever," Lily said.

"Me too, sweetie!" Dad agreed. "'Now, let's go get Mom and your brother and do a wholesome recreational activity together!"

God has set a standard for us to follow that will bring us the greatest happiness in this life and for eternity. If we can help instill righteous desires in our children, and "let this desire work in [them]," that desire will guide their decisions throughout their life. (Alma 32:27)

"Therefore what we insistently desire, over time, is what we will eventually become and what we will receive in eternity."

— Neal A. Maxwell, "According to the Desire of Our Hearts," Ensign, Nov. 1996 22,21

"Desires dictate our priorities, priorities shape our choices, and choices determine our actions. The desires we act on determine our changing, our achieving, and our becoming."

— Dallin H. Oaks, "Desire," Ensign, May 2011, 42

Life doesn't always go as we planned, even when we do all that we can do to live righteously and desire that which is good. The Lord looks upon the desires of our hearts and we will never be denied a blessing as long as we keep striving.

Ideas for teaching and memorizing
THE FAMILY: A PROCLAMATION TO THE WORLD

Choose one ingredient each week from God's recipe for a happy family and focus on it as a family.

- Faith
- Prayer
- Repentance
- Forgiveness
- Respect
- Love
- Compassion
- Work
- Wholesome recreational activities

Have Dad spend time with his sons, showing examples of presiding, providing and protecting in love and righteousness.

Have Mom spend time with her daughters, showing examples of nurturing and teaching her family.

Then, show hands-on examples, with the children together, of how to help each other "as equal partners" in those divine responsibilities.
(For families with different circumstances, give your children opportunities to learn skills from a trusted adult.)

Guess each temple! (answers at the bottom)

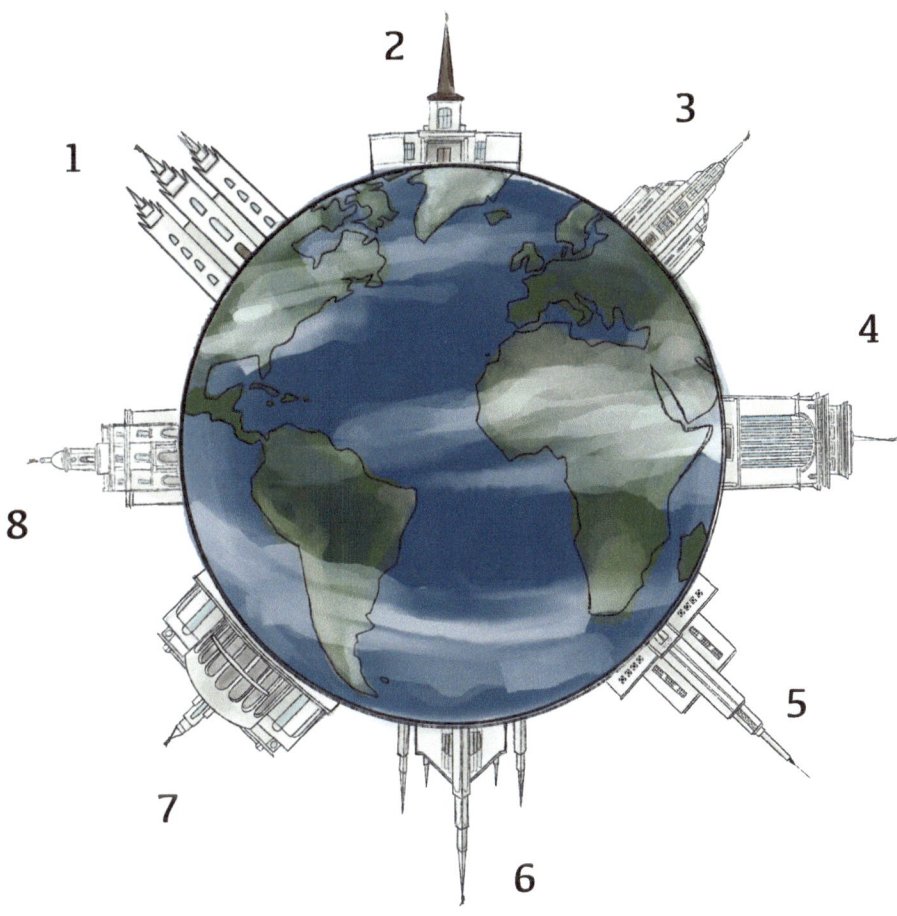

Discuss how "the divine plan of happiness enables family relationships to be perpetuated beyond the grave" by visiting a family history center and discovering and teaching about ancestors that have gone before.

Then visit the temple and share your testimony of the temple and the work done inside.

For families with older children, take names to the temple for baptisms for the dead.

For families with adult children, plan a temple trip to do endowments or sealings with family names.

1. Salt Lake City, USA   2. Helsinki, Finland   3. Rome, Italy   4. Hong Kong   5. Hamilton, New Zealand   6. Manila, Philippines   7. Recife, Brazil   8. Barranquilla, Colombia

Memorizing the Proclamation will internalize these important truths in the hearts of families. Take a paragraph, or part of a paragraph and have each member of the family draw a picture to depict each phrase. Combine them together to give visual clues to aid in the memorization of that paragraph. Place the pictures and words in a prominent place in the home, like the fireplace hearth. Have the family recite the paragraph each day during scripture study until it is memorized.

Plan a family reward for memorizing the entire Proclamation, or even just one paragraph, according to the different needs of your individual family.

As a family, research those running for public office and where they stand on issues regarding the family. Discuss who you are voting for and why.

Make a treat as a family and bring it to a family that is different than yours. Share with your children your testimony that God loves everyone no matter what their family looks like.

Acknowledgements

I want to thank my daughter, Kimball, for her immense talent and countless hours spent illustrating this book. The art is more amazing than I could ever have hoped. I also want to thank my daughter, Rylee. She was by my side through the whole process, from storyboarding, to editing, typesetting, and additional artwork. She sacrificed her time for this important project, even though she was stretched so thin with writing her own fantasy book, illustrating a children's book series and taking care of her two children, whose cuteness is off the charts. To these two wonderful daughters I give my most heartfelt gratitude.

www.ingramcontent.com/pod-product-compliance
Lightning Source LLC
Chambersburg PA
CBHW041410010526
44107CB00015B/1130